BOOKS BY

REYNOLDS PRICE

THE LAWS OF ICE   1986

KATE VAIDEN   1986

PRIVATE CONTENTMENT   1984

MUSTIAN   1983

VITAL PROVISIONS   1982

THE SOURCE OF LIGHT   1981

A PALPABLE GOD   1978

EARLY DARK   1977

THE SURFACE OF EARTH   1975

THINGS THEMSELVES   1972

PERMANENT ERRORS   1970

LOVE AND WORK   1968

A GENEROUS MAN   1966

THE NAMES AND FACES OF HEROES   1963

A LONG AND HAPPY LIFE   1962

THE LAWS OF ICE

REYNOLDS PRICE

THE LAWS OF ICE

NEW YORK

ATHENEUM

1987

Some of these poems appeared, in earlier forms, in the following places:

THE ARCHIVE   *I Am Transmuting; Midnight*
NEW LETTERS   *Before the Flood*
THE NEW YORKER   *The Claim; Rincón 2*
THE ONTARIO REVIEW   *Porta Nigra*
PALAEMON PRESS   *Lines of Life*
PHOSPHENES   *Dead Man, Dying Girl*
POETRY   *Ambrosia; Hawk Hill; A Heaven for Elizabeth Rodwell, My Mother; Lighthouse, Mosquito Inlet; Rincón 1; Three Secrets*
SHENANDOAH   *Epitaphs; Last Conversation; Remembering Golden Bells; Sleeper in the Valley*
SOUTHERN REVIEW   *For James Dean; For Leontyne Price; For Vivien Leigh*
TRIQUARTERLY   *House Snake*

Published simultaneously in Canada by Collier Macmillan Canada, Inc.
ISBN 0-689-11859-7 (clothbound); ISBN 0-689-11861-9 (paperback)
LCCN 86-47698
Composition and printing by Heritage Printers, Inc., Charlotte, North Carolina
Bound by Kale/Bindex, Inc., Charlotte, North Carolina
Designed by Harry Ford
10 9 8 7 6 5 4 3 2

CONTENTS

PRAISE   viii

O N E

AMBROSIA   3
WHAT IS GODLY   6
GOOD PLACES   7
   1.   WARM SPRINGS   7
   2.   RINCÓN 1   8
   3.   RINCÓN 2   9
   4.   CHEROKEE   11
   5.   LIGHTHOUSE, MOSQUITO INLET   12
   6.   HAWK HILL   13
BEFORE THE FLOOD   14
   1.   HER CHOICE   14
   2.   HIS DISCOVERY   15
DROWNED   16
JONATHAN'S LAMENT FOR DAVID   17
DAVID'S LAMENT FOR SAUL AND JONATHAN   19
PORTA NIGRA   20
LAST CONVERSATION   21
REMEMBERING GOLDEN BELLS   23
DEAD MAN, DYING GIRL   24
SLEEPER IN THE VALLEY   25
A HEAVEN FOR ELIZABETH RODWELL, MY MOTHER   26
EPITAPHS   31
THE LAWS OF ICE   32

T W O : D A Y S   A N D   N I G H T S

PREFACE   35
   1.   SALAMANDER   36
   2.   FLOOD   37
   3.   COOL   38

Contents

4.	HMMMM	39
5.	LUNA	40
6.	LETTER MAN	41
7.	RELIC	42
8.	PRAISE ON YOUR BIRTHDAY	43
9.	HECATOMB	44
10.	WARNED	45
11.	A POLAR SIMPLE	46
12.	RIDDLE	47
13.	THE AIM	48
14.	SAME ROAD	49
15.	LATE	50
16.	EELS	51
17.	FOR VIVIEN LEIGH	52
18.	SECRET	54
19.	FOR LEONTYNE PRICE	55
20.	CAUGHT	56
21.	CAW	57
22.	TRANSATLANTIC	58
23.	A LIFE IN DREAMS	59
24.	REST	60
25.	FOR JAMES DEAN	61
26.	THE CLAIM	62
27.	TV	64
28.	NEIGHBORS	65
29.	PEARS	66
30.	VISION	67
31.	THE DREAM OF REFUSAL	68
32.	OCTOBER SUN	70
33.	MOTHER	71
34.	TURN	72
35.	LATE VISIT	73

THREE

LINES OF LIFE	77
THREE SECRETS	78

1. JOSEPH   78
2. MARY   81
3. JESUS   82

ROAD   86

THREE VISITS   87
1. DIONYSOS   87
2. APHRODITE   91
3. HERMES PSYCHOPOMPOS   94

YOUR BLOOD   97

HELIX   98

I AM TRANSMUTING   99

A TOMB FOR WILL PRICE   100

MIDNIGHT   103

HOUSE SNAKE   104

WATCHMAN. TOWER. MIDNIGHT.   116

PRAISE

Holy flame
By any name—
Creator, Terminator,
   Hand—

Receive this praise,
The due of days
Of hobbled terror, healing:
   Thanks.

Your muffled light,
Its comrade night
Swept outward, forward, farther
   Home.

ONE

AMBROSIA

The hard part, I grant, in being a god is standing
Still to bear the worship—enduring the leach
Of dilate eyes, incessant frisk of adoring
Hands: meals of the blind.
                        In defense, most gods
Extrude some cast of themselves as durable adequate
Receptacles of awe—a seal on the air of one
Patently suitable place from the unplumbed
Intaglio absence of their force:
                              chryselephantine Zeus
At Olympia, dog-dugged Artemis at Ephesus—freeing
Their essences to vagabond the landscape, debauching briny
Island lads or booming the birthrate in crossroad hamlets
(Six glorious girls and a brackish well),
Triggering outbreaks of scabies or earthquakes or six months'
Boreal splendors at sunset or sulks on their tripods
At final subjection to dread bronze Necessity.

Of you, when the live body takes its furloughs,
There is just this thickening sheaf of photographs
(Coaxed by me, peeled off your presence) and this one
Cranium's smoky memorial corroborations
Of the radiant claims incredible in monochrome—
The days during years in which for hours there would settle
Upon you or burn from within a packed imperative
I am goal and terminus, first and last. What
In the world shines or refuses is chargeable to me,
All thanks all blame. Choose which, kneel here, enact
Your choice.
                  In the body's vicinity, its transpirations,
My prompt enactments have mostly seemed thanks (though you've
Suggested the occasional oblation was clandestine management,
Puppetry)—the thanks of, say, a mature self-
Possessed English setter at dusk who swabs

The master's nutritious hand in transports of service
Pure as the moon's sucking gaze at the sea and rapt
As the heart of stalwart Gabriel in rainbow gear
Lobbing pitch-perfect glories at the Thunder Throne.

—Which raises the unbrushed but omnipresent
God above Necessity, ireful desert
Yahweh, El Shaddai, who's made a long
Point of vouchsafing no image and whose
High shrine was an unlit cubicle empty
Of all but a wood box holding two rock
Slabs with rules for fleeing Egypt
(And maybe the conduct of stationary lives throughout
Our universe till Hell reopens as an ice-skating rink)—
The second rule forbidding surmise at his face,
Other efficacious organs.
                              Yet—
This is crucial—recall we're built
Precisely "in his image, after his likeness." Assume
We are. Then each is an ample portable altar
For any other's holocaust;
                              and what I silently
Say to you—presence not pictures
Though they may yet serve—in hour-long veneration
Bouts (when, thoughtless as a sponge, I roam you minutely
Companioned by orts of pleasure in a voice I take
On faith to be yours transforming) is my best
Equation of the offering earned by palpable data.
I choose you again. Vulnerable ramparts—
Blood, oil, water, effulgent crowns
Of crackling hair, ten local odors distinct
As dialects—sufficient idol of absolute
Stillness, motion, making, annihilation.

So, at ease. Enjoy each instant of this. Never think
You're alone. I'm also Adam and thus another
Mold however botched of the Convex Love that monitors black
Holes, cheerleader contests, the footwork of quarks,
Famines in the Punjab. With logic and full right

I incorporate for a hundredth time the excess
You yield—copious sacrament, feast of gods,
Which I turn to good.

WHAT IS GODLY

What is godly
This moment
Is the sight of you,
Promise of indelible memory
Of the sight—
Motionless heave
Of vertical body
On bone-white wall
In October light, slant
But gilding—
                what has been
Godly ten unquestioned years.

GOOD PLACES

1. WARM SPRINGS

We think we've come here to start
A life or that figure of life
Neither of us has drawn: closed
Circle, live circuit.
Initial trials have suggested
Feasibility (quick congruences
In your house and mine);
So we take us on the road through July
Mountains to this enormous
Round pool in a valley, warm
As we, for the first attempt
On public ground.

Jefferson bathed here, R. E. Lee;
Centuries of Indians, vatic lustrations;
Protestant dynasties of hearts,
Livers, reins.
We strip, descend, and water
Receives us—no Tantalus-flight—
Enlisting to serve, plating
Our entire pelts with air:
A zillion beads of adhesive buoyance.
We may levitate!—glide
The ridge on thermals till night,
Nude as eggs.

Why then do you whisper "Watch this,"
Exhale and sink—white
Plummet—to the green cobble
Floor, untouchable corpse
Twitched by currents gentler than my hand?

And why do you rise?

2. RINCÓN 1

You wake each dawn and silently leave
Me in our dank room beside an ocean
Calm as custard and drive our rented
Car through a village posing for the start
Of a John Huston movie—louche
Alleys, cantinas with oneeyed cats.
In two green miles you reach the north
Cape, the squat-globe *planta nuclear*—
Effluent warming the warm Caribbean
To a half-mile shark-cafeteria,
Waves the best in the hemisphere
For your present purpose. You launch your board
And paddle to the break a hundred yards
Out where eight baked blankface
Earlybirds from the hippie surfer colony
That camps in the hills all winter refuse
You—glares meaningless as toads'.

                                        I sleep
And dream houses, a child hunting
Houses.
              You plane in, roll after roll, perfect
Rider in the element that grants
You triumph—sentient sea.

On the beach a fatboy hometown
Liberationist in Che Guevara tam
Dreams of slicing you down with automatic fire.
Failing that, he watches. You are not unseen.

3. RINCÓN 2

Christmas eve afternoon in the hot toy
Plaza, beer—me learning
Lycidas, you coaching my lines,
We apparently invisible: no passer,
Woman or child, concedes us.

Dinner on the cliff by the suicide curve,
Tropical lobster (all tail),
Men's room with a ripped-off basin
Trembling on its pipes. Vast sight
Of the sea, calm lid on "the bottom
Of the monstrous world"; outrageous stars.

Our first midnight mass since Vatican II
In the glum beige church swarmed
Solid—steady jolts: no syllable
Of Latin, dignified slab-altar hung
In carcinogenic colors, whiskered
Ladies at ease in the chancel
Machine-gunning dialect scripture
Grim as death lists.
                    A summit
When a prepubescent boy and girl
Advance in white, kneel, embed
The shocking-pink Child in actual
Straw as a man in azure leisure-
Suit squats to flip a loud switch—red
Lights wink antiphonal relays on the stable
Roof.
          We think it's over now; our eyes
Think *Sleep.* Our neighbors in the crush,
Men with horn farmer-necks, spread
Barrel arms and seize us; you laugh

"We're mugged!" Dry kisses at our ears;
Then standoff faces again, quarter-smiles,
Intermittent tan teeth; their hardwon salutation
Spent on tall pale strangers.

Well, we bear its health back
And sustain it three days.

4. CHEROKEE

For my day on the roads
In your direction
(Last two hours
On wounded-snake
Blue Ridge ascents,
Eating lilac monoxide
From not-quite-stalled
Road-crazed oldtimers
In campers equipped
For Armageddon),
You offer this—

Half-hour warmup
Before the show;
Dancers worked
Like puppets in oil
By Tchaikovsky's *Serenade*
For Strings, such grave
Jubilation; you
Unhurried on the dim
Periphery, trainee
Mover:

Dazzling enactment,
Crystal grown
By the music's glut,
Its durable reward
And mine, six years.

5. LIGHTHOUSE, MOSQUITO INLET

If we'd stood here in this upthrust lantern
Eighty-six years ago, staring east through eyes
As officious as these we've turned on each other, we'd have seen
The steamer *Commodore* (out of Jacksonville
With guns for Cuba) sink just there, a tidy
Knot in the hectic juncture of water, sky; then an all but
Phantom spot start toward us at the rate of roots
In basalt—Stephen Crane and four men in a ten-foot
Dinghy yearning toward us, this light at least,
What they can see of a shore craved ardently as heart's ease
At sunset (the sun will desert them on its compulsive chore,
The lid of the known world lock on their faces,
Lips eat frigid salt a whole night
From unseen whelms—January 1897).
None of them knows the color of the sky.

Our day, a late November noon, is likewise
A woodcut in gray and gray—though (safe in the glass
At the close of a jaunt distinguished, I feel, for torpid
Bliss; posing you against a sea glum
As a rattler in a roadside cage), I hardly guess
We are also scuttled by the silent insatiable bit
Of your fear: dread precisely of proximate safety,
Harmless salvage. In an hour you're to fly north,
Weapon stowed in a skull Etruscan in numinous vapidity.
The strength of its seams invisibly compressing a craze
More urgent than your plane's for flight. My adjacent blindness
Is the noon's chief glow—rays from a hope perennial
As sleet, sufficient to stoke me and blaze strangers on.
Flee in it, well-lit (a final gift), your shadow
Flung forward, no backward stain.
You at least know the color of the sky—
Ashen for waste, jaundice for lies.

6. HAWK HILL

August dusk. We rest on the green porch,
Yellowjackets and ants at our knees—
You in from work, ready to cook
The dinner I can't; I three-fourths through
The eightieth sick-day, weaker still;
We cheering a milestone with smooth Glenlivet:
Eleven years of peace and war,
Our squalls and calms. The hidden thrush
In the big beech behind us pauses to plan
His billionth variation on the five notes
Stamped in his throat.
                    You face me and say
"*Real time,*" then add with customary
Unbarked candor "Whether you make it
Or not, these days were real time"—
Twelve days in which you've fed me squarely,
Dried my bedsore, each night stripped
My slack legs for baby-sleep (that sound and brief):
No word or sign of balk or grievance,
The flawless service dreamed by kings.

Whether I make it or not, old struggler
(Treasured as any, with all our scars),
Feel it hereafter as all real time—
All one linked try to tread one void.
We pay for it now.

The angels saw that women were lovely and took wives for themselves
GENESIS 6

BEFORE THE FLOOD

1. HER CHOICE

My sisters and I were climbing from the spring,
So we moved slow and upright—no drop wasted.
The ground had been dry but cool when we went;
Now it blistered with each careful step but I
Couldn't stop. I was leading, the tallest.
The Earth herself was famished, begging mercy.
I thought we might each splash a few drops.
                                        He
Rose in the path, a silent shout—from earth
Or air itself, I never saw. I lurched enough
To spill a whole drink; my sisters managed
To save their pitchers but fell and hid
Their eyes.
            His face was the single face I'd
Dreamed. The eyes, the brown space between
And beneath them, were a whole world I'd mapped
And prowled at night. His body was dense and
Lean as a bench, entirely bare. Where a man's
Sex is, he grew a third hand—long clean
Fingers with thick ivory nails. It reached
Upward on him but was still as the light.

It was why I went to him, why I gave him
My whole firm body to rummage like a strong
Blind beggar for what seemed life. His
Eyes never shut.

2. HIS DISCOVERY

What I found up in her—
Not the fluid complicity
Of celestial hydraulics,
Grave conjugation
Of stainless souls
But a nubby palpable
Compact relief-map
(Canyons and foothills;
A tan savanna)
Of a county with rough
Tongues and hardy scrub timber;
Chinked huts at intervals
To slow an enemy
And children at low doors
In stairsteps of age:
Brown, oiled,
And skittish in
A dark that baited,
Welcomed, eased
Me more than
Guaranteed endless
Silent billows
Of curative shine.

DROWNED

The hour strikes and staves our hull.
Crack of night, fate founders,
Famished storm whelms flesh and wine.
And I (all man) groan, calculate.
My mind's too keen, too fit to watch
Time's brittle hourglass destroyed.
The deep and I are one machine
For scrounging littered memories—
Mother, my china cups, the whore
Greased and throbbing on the lurid sill,
And Christ! See Christ there lashed to the mast
Jigging to death in pitchdark salt.
His bloody eye flares one last sign—
A great ship perished, all hands drowned.

after Paul Valéry

When David returned from the slaughter of the Philistine, Abner took him and brought him before Saul with the Philistine's head in his hand.

Saul said to him "Whose son are you?"

David answered "I'm the son of your servant Jesse the Bethlehemite."

It happened when he'd finished speaking to Saul that Jonathan's soul was knit with David's soul. Jonathan loved him like his own soul.

1 SAMUEL 17: 57–18: 1

JONATHAN'S LAMENT FOR DAVID

You young in the bronze day, gore to the wrists,
Coarse hair kinked in the cold sweat of triumph,
Thrusting the startled head at Father
(Pumpkin-huge with turquoise earbobs,
Chinking bells), you rank with the first wild
Stench of manhood roasting your fork—
It happened I loved you, watched my heart
Fling thin cords past the grinning giant
And bind you in; watched yours bind me:
Safe in the first and strongest bond.

You were fourteen, herdboy still.
I was nineteen, prince and heir.
I'd prided myself on self-possession.
In the wheedling murderous alleys of court,
I'd owned my own soul, long-thewed body—
No man's boy to fetch and carry,
No milky girl's to trap and tame.
A love to outrun love of girls—

We only flourished, fed by glare
Of priests' eyes—king's and cringing slaves'—
The packed hot floors of muffled rooms,
Cool caves, dry bivouac beds on rock.
The first taut cords of meeting eyes
Became twined legs and hands, locked lips,
Pooled opal seed we planted deep—
Buried to bloom in secret night,
Public deeds of sunstruck valor.
Love past woman's love or God's

And proved through daily fierce onslaught—
Palace, tent, every hand,
Father's envy, Samuel's rage,
Our blank despair at shrinking ground
On which to join and feed again
This single-stalked bent desert tree
We bred to last on air and night.
Love past every human love

Till now you rise in gilding light
And stretch your brown blunt victor's arms;
Assume the bleached dense marriage-shirt
To take my sister, your first bride—
Grinning head thrust ruddy toward me,
Swapping me for one pale girl
(My nursery-mate, your throneward path).

This love—gazelle to bound all crags—
Breaks, gored, on thorns of our killed tree.

DAVID'S LAMENT FOR SAUL AND JONATHAN

Gazelle of Israel slain on the heights
The mighty fallen

Conceal it in Gath and Ashkelon's alleys
Or the daughters of the Philistine rejoice
Daughters of the vile uncut exult

Hills in Gilboa no dew no rain no harvest fields
The shield of the mighty grimed with dust
The shield of Saul stained unready

From gore of the slain from warrior fat
The bow of Jonathan turned not back
Sword of Saul returned not hungry

Saul and Jonathan loved and lovely
Unparted in life in death unparted
Past eagles swift past lions strong

Daughters of Israel weep for Saul
Who decked you in crimson hung you with gold
The mighty fallen in midst of war

Jonathan slain upright on the heights
I mourn you brother too dear for me
Your love fell on me spring of wonder
Past all women's love and wonder

The mighty fallen
The arms of war

after David

PORTA NIGRA

Why wake me to watch you rule the world?—
I who watched the grandest days of Treves,
Paired in fame with her one sister Rome.
These eyes have burned with flare of clattering legions,
Blond Franks bled by lions in the sand,
Trumpets at the palace and the god
Augustus purple in his golden car;
Have rested happy in my river home
(Ringed by shouts as grapes were pulped to wine)
On girls who lifted jars tumid with life.

    And now you rouse me to blank rubble fields,
Shards of walls nightly licked by fog,
Sacred statues blasphemed in their graves
By what you dig above them—slews for swine.

    Only my lovely gate stands undefiled.
Hung with black swags of time, it still flings scorn
On your squat roofs, squat backs, from every hole;
On princes, vassals, priests—each in his mask
(Alike, jowls bloated, flaccid grin, blind stare)—
On women my drunk slaves would not gang-rape.

    What diet do you drain from breasts of junk?
The only precious thing has fled you—blood.
We shadows still remember streaming fire.

    "Live corpses!" laughs the boy Manlius;
"I would not rule such men even with this rod
That hooked my bread when—oiled with Persian musk—
Each night I prowled our dim triumphal gate;
Sold my lean self to Caesar's own bought men."

after Stefan George

LAST CONVERSATION *(Joel Jackson, 1945–1980)*

One of the comfort-stops
In my adolescence, grim
As the War of the Spanish Succession
And some years longer,
Was the laughing home your parents
Made—you the readiest
Laugher. At three or four
You sang me "Little Oyster,"
Eight-second song
That became our rune.

Little Oyster went to school.
He couldn't learn the Golden Rule.

Had you made it up?
Or heard it right?—the leakage,
The stench! Was it maybe "Oscar"?
"Oyster" it stayed, though,
The rest of your life;
My name for you.

The week you died, I sat by your bed—
Noon July murk, fresh
Tacos in the yard, muttering friends,
You and I alone, you
A flung sack of bones, mind
Burning unpredictably in and
Out of service. I strained to think
What to ask if you looked up again
And knew my face—something
Idle enough to spare you work
But earn me credit for a visit
Than which I'd have rather drunk slugs
Of battery acid. In minutes your eyes goggled

Round, me the target. I said
"Whyever did I call you 'Little Oyster'?"
And thought I knew the answer. You could no
Longer smile, only groan "Goddamn"
To signal surprise; so your answer was slow
But Delphic in closure—"You used
To say the world was my oyster."

Did I? I recall no prophecy,
Though the far skirts of doom are among
My bigger lines. The world
Anyhow took five more days
To eat you.
                    Is the pearl of that
Long transaction swelling
Now?

REMEMBERING GOLDEN BELLS

Disgraced and sick, a man age forty.
Oblivious and straight, a girl age three—
Not a son but enough to ease odd moments,
The occasional kiss. Then they lured her ghost
Who knows where?
                              Remembering how,
The week she died, she groped for words
To tell me news, I learned that gambles
On flesh only win me desolation.
Thinking to times before her though,
I sealed out pain.
                              Three years now
Since my heart froze, each day of three winters.
This morning—spring—the grief ran free.
On the warm street I met her old nurse.

after Po Chu-i

DEAD MAN, DYING GIRL *(Robert Kennedy, 1925–1968)*

In England—bored one Sunday, '61—
I spent two minutes staring at your face,
Photograph cast up in that day's news.
Staring because you seemed (baffling then,
Two years pre-Dallas) trapped in silent woe;
And just two minutes, what it took to see
The principle of line that signaled pain.
Your eyes, not straight, rushed downward from your nose;
Watershed beneath a simian brow—
Eyes of my friend Kaufman, Lew Hoad's eyes,
Petrified dumb masks of Greece and Rome,
Stock-in-trade of subsequent cartoons:
Lines sloping downward indicate real pain.

But seven years farther in—you freshly killed—
I see your eyes, no continental ridge
Or open sockets drilled in howling mask,
And see they tie you to another head—
The Boston Museum's marble girl of Chios.
She works to smile but fails. Now I know why.
Face still trembles pure, three thousand years;
Skull remains unfinished, sides rush down—
To bear a mantle, all the guidebooks say;
Cloth to roof her beauty, name her fate:
Bride in white led out to meet a life
Or thistle wool to warm a colder way.
She waits on there in Boston your raw home,
Not yet quite living—needy, bare, no mantle.

Yours has descended, spared at least the wait.

SLEEPER IN THE VALLEY

A green hole in the hills, a river sings
Clutching a path through weeds like torn drowned silver.
Blank noon sun takes steady aim and flings;
Spent rays converge here, arrows in a quiver.

A soldier—young, mouth open, naked head,
Bathing his hair in fresh blue watercress—
Stretches at ease beneath pale roofing cloud,
Bedded in raining glare on deep green grass.

His feet are in sword flowers, across his nap
A sick child's smile is creased. Rocked in earth's lap,
Pelted by warming light, still he is cold

And flares no answer to the heavy scent
Of day. He sleeps, one hand in silent fold
Of chest. Two red holes in his side. Here on the right.

after Arthur Rimbaud

A HEAVEN FOR ELIZABETH RODWELL,
MY MOTHER

Each morning her mother does not die.
It is always August; she's eleven years old,
Her father comes toward her in the far bedroom
Which is already shuttered against a sun dry
As a fired brick-kiln. She's clean,
Dressed, ready, seated on her bed, and has prayed
He will not come—that someway the room
Will answer the sucking light, tear free, and rush
(She's been nowhere, can think of no refuge—
Sky bottomless sky?). Her father reaches
The mat by the bed and touches a spot
On the crown of her scalp that has been sore six years—
She fell backward, laughing at a joke
Of the cook's, from a kitchen window and tore a short
Mouth in the fishbelly-skin round which
Coarse hair already darkened. Now he says
"*Your mother needs to speak to you.*" Elizabeth
Rises, sustaining his palm, a helmet on her brain;
And says "*Is she going to die today?*"
Her father nods and leads her through the only house
She's lived in—Jack Rodwell, matrix
Of her dark eyes and hair; his own hair stiff
As hemp, still mostly raven. The front
Bedroom is bright but cool; her brothers have sent
For two huge blocks of ice—they melt
In galvanized tubs by unscreened windows. There are three
Brothers, all grown by the bed—
Three older sisters—a clutch of inlaws, a Negro
Nurse, the young useless doctor.
They make a slow aisle; and her father draws
Her down it, damp miles to the bed.
It is white iron and high, the mattress butts
Her windpipe, her eyes—mottled bronze—

Are in a thin plane with her mother's hip.
Her mother—Lizzie—stout for years,
Is bloating unstoppably instant by instant with the refuse
Of a short hard jocular life,
An early good marriage, eight children (one
Dead), and forty-eight years: now
Bright's disease, ruined kidneys, poison
Lapping at her eyes. But she can still
See. She faces Elizabeth, a skewed right
Angle; and though she does not intend it,
Grins in the sodden pleats of a mouth that was sweet
As wings days ago. Then she says "I *meant*
To see you through. You're the one I'll miss." Boots,
The sissy brother, blubs. Elizabeth
Nods once, sips ammoniac air, and bites down
Gently on a fold of sheeting, the nearest
Refuge. A thought speaks, keen in her head as a blade—
This is making me an orphan. This is all against
Me. Her father takes her left wrist,
Awkwardly turns her. She staggers away,
Mute as she came, to lie on her own bed—
Far too big—and wait for a life
If a life volunteers. Then her mother does not die.
The cook bears the message, tall Mary Green—
Mopping her own eyes with sugar-sack apron
And hands like leather primeval birds—
"*Your mother all right. Or going to be. She
Last till you stop needing her.
Get up and run.*" Elizabeth believes it (Mary Green
Is one thing here that's never lied)
And stands like a cold pony loath to work,
Then strides into this new life I provide—
Full August noon, an endless furnace,
That does her no harm.

Each afternoon her husband takes her,
Standing on the beige tile floor of his toilet
In Rex Hospital where he waits for tomorrow
When they'll split his huge chest in search of tumors

That may be the murk scumbled over
His X-rays, blundering hands. Not hers—
Hers by their silent presence, still
As objects, on his cold bedsheet have summoned this rite
For survival in a body hefty as a grown
Tree, bone-tan and precious in her mind more than half
Her life till now; cause of food,
Two sons, a stillborn daughter, the customary
Rages, all the safety and recompense she's known
To this day. February 16th, a day
Like a broad glass pane onto nothing but
Cold; she turned forty-nine nine
Days ago. She cooperates to the bounds
Of her still perdurable strength as she's done (barring
Helpless failures by her body) for twenty-
Seven years since their first night, bare
In the rickety dark of a Pullman grinding
To Tampa Bay for their one sustained stretch
Of unblocked access before quick thickets
Of tollgates descended between their flesh and where
It aimed to go—entire conjunction,
Inseparable compound of self in self, companioned
Only by grateful laughter and the requisite
Mercies toward whatever ambient life might prowl
The nutrient glow of their steadfast blaze.
William—still Will, eyes still
Hot as brands though gray as his hair:
He's half a head taller and must buckle to root
His broad way into the place he never
Thinks about—warm as his mother, more dreamless than sleep.
Bucking on his long calves, he does not
Think but rests for maybe the final time. She
Braces and thinks *This will kill me too.*
In a minute I'll flood with cancer. She sees it—chalk
White and fitted with irresistible
Baby-claws that will score their way to her heart
By spring. Yet she keeps strict time
With her own strong hips, assisting him deeper
Into fragile shelters he's never found

Before. He asks *"Is it right?"* for the four thousandth
Time, she moans at his neck, he floods
In apparently endless gouts—scrubbing her forehead
With a sharkhide chin. Now he always
Thanks her, she waits, he's silent. She thinks
He knows he's infected me. She thinks
I cannot bear to hear him beg pardon;
So she stops him by saying her own lucid
"Thank you" and pulling back, free. Only then—
Slow as finding home in a nightmare
And richer in joy—she sees it's cured him; she's
Cured him: her sad compliant skin.
In the glint of his new health, his first face
(Simple and stunning as a hill in cloudless
Outrage of sun), she forgets her own doom,
Saying as she grins and joins him again
"You'll outlast me. Dress. We're leaving here."
He thanks her at last.

Each night she dies under expert watch—
Intensive Care—in Wake County Hospital;
Surprisingly eager to quit this course
She's run sixty years, ravenous hunt
Through familiar ground—occasional ambush,
Uncharted voids: no halt for pain.
The right carotid artery behind
Her eyes ruptured at five o'clock; and she
Was brought here, unable to speak,
Apparently senseless, her brain already so crushed
By blood as to be past all known help
But witness. The breathing proximity she lent me through dozens
Of childhood nights (barking croup, dreams
Of flight) is now repaid in a single sum,
Ruinous speed. But shutdown though
She appallingly seems, she files my presence; makes
It the token to trip mired cogs
Of easement; they grind this last lean wish—
Her first son (me) will leave now,
Freeing her to end among strangers: brusque dry

A Heaven for Elizabeth Rodwell, My Mother

Mercy on white rubber soles,
Prowling her border, an arm's reach away
If the arm could reach (her only other
Son is becalmed on a Navy scow
Off bristling Cuba). I accept then and stand,
A last obedience but hedged with scruples, imperfect
Service. I have this last chance
To lay up sights to see me through maybe
Four more decades of memory. Do I want
An album of angles on a stout lady swamping
Silently beneath a weak glow?
The only relief, an uncurtained window
On a May-night storm, air itself
Gorged on its own warm sap. Then I see the change that,
Stunned, I've missed—she's somehow flying.
The gullies of her shut face are leveled, swept
Back by a rush down something, toward
Something. The goal is stripping years off her,
Stale padding. She will soon be
Her first self, the girl before me;
Not dreaming of me; not subject
To sons, husband, parents, a life. I have this
Last chance she speeds to deny me.
I take three quick steps into chill
Light, she's almost arrived, her wake is
Diaphanous. I touch the mattress, lift a seersucker spread,
A leaden sheet, and find her blue
Hand—startling and expected like teeth
In a dig, wire-thin platinum wedding-ring
On the prescribed finger. With my nail I nick it—
Chip-diamonds, half-lost; little black mouths of absence.
It wobbles to my touch, loose on its knuckle.
I remove it easily. She knows, thinks *No*, imagines
She's said it. I slip it on the outside finger
Of my left hand, firm safe fit.
She thinks *Yes. Go.*

EPITAPHS FROM THE GREEK ANTHOLOGY

1. You gaze at stars, my star—that I were skies,
   To gaze at you with endless billion eyes.

   after Plato

2. I'm dead. For all I care
   The world can melt. I smile.

   Anonymous

3. All of Zosima that slaved
   Was her body. That's free.

   after Damascius the Philosopher

4. I lie under this now—
   The famous woman who lay for one man.

   Anonymous

5. This is where Philippus buried
   His twelve-year-old son Nicoteles, his hope.

   after Callimachus

THE LAWS OF ICE

Ice has laws
(Oxygen, fire,
Lord Gravity
Have laws) but loose—
A mother's call.

Human life
(Yours, mine)
Will glide down decades
Free as oil;

Then seize on the instant,
Rigid form—
Your statue, mine,
Perfected ice:

Random pose,
Appalling laws.

TWO

TWO

DAYS AND NIGHTS

A JOURNAL

On 13 February 1984 I began a notebook in which I meant to write short poems that sketched actual events of my days and nights (events that are often invisible—thoughts, reflexes, dreams; the dreams here are plain transcriptions).

From the first I attempted a tone that was brisk and supple, sufficiently Horatian to permit both the minutiae of a diary and more sizable concerns. Always I aimed to walk the charged line that divides the territories of poetry and prose, with only the requisite tacks to right or left—the flat-lit grasslands of prose, the jagged uplands of verse.

The fact that many of the impulses came in sonnet forms was a surprise and, for me, the confirmation of an old suspicion—that the shape of the sonnet participates in a near-metabolic unity with the western mind's rate of experience and reflection.

When I began I had no expectation of the catastrophe that would announce itself on 2 June, but subliminal warnings sound as early as number 21 (3 April). The remaining entries confront the aftermath, through 14 February 1985.

Here are all the attempts of that year. None was retouched after the day or two in which it was still malleable, though in deference to a friend's privacy, I have altered two words.

DAYS AND NIGHTS

1. SALAMANDER

Sun—in the belly of February—and through
The hot pane, a motorized tiller eats
The old garden: basil stalks, wet gourds,
Hulls of our summer like rented Heaven:
Maybe six harsh words (all mine).
                                        A week ago,
Snow; and I led you out eighteen miles of ice
Through cars abandoned like tanks to an airport
Crazy as Lisbon 1940 and left you
To slice your own lean way to new summer—lions!
The meat-chocked plains.
                                Have you yet faced west?—northwest
Toward here? Next time, remember to face the ground.
Concede the earth's curve. I might be in Hell.
You might be, from where I face down here.

Grin back. Adore the flame.

2. FLOOD

Full moon in three days, and last night black rain
In deafening sheets all round whatever sleep I got.
Through it, rags of dream—each a flash of you:
Outside, unshielded, upright in the roar
On the dam of the pond in phosphorous glare,
Both arms at your sides, palms curled toward me
(Strontium chunks), face blank as bread but fixed
On mine with lidless eyes.
                                    This morning, calm—
Pond at bankful, the creek a torrent—
I grope toward day, stunned as any drowned rock.
No way to know if I've prophesied, *seen*, or staged
The millionth tableau of punitive dread—
Me flailing me for excess joy
In my old toy theater, endless night-court.

3. COOL

The tenants fire-up their burglar alarm, then rush
To a party—forgetting the antique dog's indoors.
Ten minutes later she trips the siren. Its Gestapo
Wow-wow bursts on my dinner. Pillaged at random
Five times myself, I creep out into the dark
Muddy field in bedroom slippers and watch their windows—
Just out of pistol range. Every chink is lit
Though shaded. *Who's there?*
                                    Mired to the ankles,
I may be watching one more loved body gutted
From the heart out, ravenous jaws.
                                    Despite the premature
Fug on the night, I stay the coolest object—
Stroked by the nine-tenths moon breaking treeline:
A menopausal diva, gone in the slats.
Splinter every board. I can watch.

4. HMMMM

Famed as you are for your trick of snoozing through direct
Two-or-more megaton strikes on your actual bed
(Or rampant prowls by me, the Dawn Unicorn), I doubt
You're fazed by tonight's moon—fulfilled, size
Of a radioactive sterling washtub hung on my chimney
And frying *me*, prone sleepless as a Wall Street ticker at noon.
    I and several billion sensitive-plants worldwide
(Including all oceans, all tectonic plates, pigs, bird-egg yolks)
Are rung tonight like tuning forks, a lunatic
Barbershop trillionet.
                        I beam my helpless tone
Your way, not knowing your way—Masai corrals
(Lapping bloodlaced milk), tawny sedge veldt, or diamond shaft
So deep in rock as to be past even this silvery suck?
    Hear my one note though, sleep refreshed.

5. LUNA

Why has no one, in no country ever, contended
You were male? The Man in the Moon was
Never you but in you, on you—idiot leer.

You want us back in you? Is that the famine
You burgeon through four weeks to glut; then phut out
Empty again, futile mensis?

—But maybe me. I've been a sentient target
Since birth. Mother's landlocked meer
Surely neaped and ebbed to your mute pull.

I still dream at least of treading in womb dark,
Dreading your draw through Mother's pink hide—
Slack-webbed to save me but bound to lose.

Vast pitiful gorgeous toothless mouth at the east pond-window,
Vast Hole Mother—this son yields finally. Now feed deep.

6. LETTER MAN

Saturday—the best in this lifeline of warm days
Flung at our heads—I was indoors of course, stripping
For a nap, when some force blammed the frontdoor glass.
Songbirds regularly dash their paper skulls
On its simulacrum of trees, berries, bugs.
So I assumed, say, one dead bluebird and
Fell on the bed. A second hit and "*Mr.*
Price" bellowed in a desperate strange voice.

Through the glass he looks like the Pale Avenger—black-
Headed, short, in a rose plaid shirt, with grainy skin,
A bowed shrunk right arm, and blank laser
Eyes.
      Helpless, reckless, I open the door.
He says "Mr. Price, can I fish your pond?" I say
"Where do you live?" (odd—not "Who are you?").
He fights a hard tremor; the dwarf arm shakes
South toward my dense woods—"That trailer
In yonder." I say "It's fished out."
He says "No it ain't."
                I've already offered my throat,
The lush baggage of my life strewn behind me. What's
Left but "Yes"? I add "Just you." Smiles
Are not in his power, but he tackles one—tormented wrench.

He's halfway gone in the throat of the woods when I see
The sign he always makes—upright spine,
Bent arm at his side: a trembling P
In the I's of the trees.
          Wracked mascot, fish for me!

7. RELIC

Your first card's here—eleven days in transit—
And you're not after all nailed to the mulchy
Swarming floor of a third-world jail, being
Flayed in elegant unbroken strips,
But are tented in candlelight thirty yards
From lions and hyenas chuckling at their feed
And have already witnessed a circumcision
In a Masai village.
              Look, six days ago
Here I guessed you might be feeding
On warm Masai cow's-milk streaked
With warmer red.
              Did they circumcise a boy or
Girl? What age and how? Who saved the blood?
Short of being speared-down in the ring by braves,
Could you have caught it in a clean white rag?

8. PRAISE ON YOUR BIRTHDAY

Edible flesh,
A leavened bread.

Eyes to watch
Your flood consume
Me, match my smile.

Mind reckless, fragrant,
Open-handed—
Alexander

By the green Hydaspes:
Elephant charge!

9. HECATOMB

Dave, a gale's slamming through from the west;
And you're at another stand, reading your high hot
Grave-eyed poems to another room of eyes.
I'm beached back here in the dim house alone,
Stove-up from our night of talk—word-oblations,
Big shoulders of each life slabbed on a communal
Altar in midair above the teak table's
Ashtrays and books: propitiations?
Rewards? Raw fuel.
                     Your son—weed-high
With a sooty lip to forecast beard—
Sat (an angle to our line, watchful as a nauga);
Then smiled my way and claimed "I've never
Seen him like this." What had we shown
Him but unendable hunger?

10. WARNED

Christmas, I gave myself a set of runes—
A softedged California guru's guess
At the lost Norse code of divination.

This morning, packing for our plan to meet
(Eight p.m., Eastern Airlines, cold Milwaukee),
I sheepishly consult the old-new signs—

Blindly drawing three from the leather pouch,
Spreading them facedown, one by one
Confronting their bleak promise, silent threat:

Signals reversed, Constraint, Movement reversed.
Crouched, I proceed as though the toys are charged—
Urim and Thummim, eyeslots onto time.

Milwaukee eight hours later, no surprise.
You fail our meeting, swear you'll come tomorrow.

11. A POLAR SIMPLE

Six times in precisely forty-eight hours
Together, half-dark, we descended the shaft
Lined with no eyes but ours; and there on the flat,
On firm yielding ground, concurred in the earnest
Minutes of strife that always end
In blinding glare of absolute joy—
Each thanking each for gifts dense
As pitchblende, discoveries startling as the polar
Crocus (eight leaves locked round
A rank flamboyant pistil) from which
Today these crucials are derived:
An imbrication for the fear of dreams,
Heartsease in ampules small as seed,
A dauntless fulminant for hope.

12. RIDDLE

Stalk that blooms in total night,
No need of eyes.

Astonishment that powders rock,
Silent as fur.

13. THE AIM

We rise from these days and walk west and east
Into thriving separate worlds blank-ignorant
Of what we've swapped on this clean bed—

Your hidden essence, tapped by pleasure;
My circling hunger to consume but spare;
Our silent pact to man this circuit

For lasting service, warming both lives
(Their adjacent towns) and lighting the acts
Of creatures undreamed of here but implicit:

Red droves of children at play on hills,
A woman sworn to tend you always,
Whatever calm stranger shuts my eyes.

The secret of fire was our main aim.
Surely we turn in its fierce candor now.

14. SAME ROAD

Twenty-five years ago—me dark and lean—
This road was only the hyphen between us,
Five hours of concrete I could roll tight
Till we joined again in roomy Georgetown,
A brick village still, you gold and gleaming.
　The highway's wallowed, devouring oaks
And crossroad stores with handmade signs
(*If you believe in credit, lend me* $5.00);
And Georgetown's crammed with clerks young enough
To be our sons, each hazed with hope
Of bone-on-bone, adhesive flesh,
Yips of joy in rooms cramped as milk cartons.
　Like us—then, now. But what we made!
Utter trust, safe decades, past shoals of thieves.

15. LATE

There are three of us, yes; but why
At the end of this courteous night
Are we posted still at three angles
Of a table by cold scraped bowls
When—huge at the window—an avid
Moon pumps white demand
To rise, dowse lights, and hoop
Our limbs on bed or floor:
Joint enactment of her
Lone unity, streaming gift?

16. EELS

From the first full letter,
This falls, first-pop;
And is thus my first sight
In five weeks, of you
—On an Afrikaans beach,
Encased in French models
(Worn as brogans,
Nude wilting tits),
You wear black trunks
You wore the day
We bobbed the Dead Sea's
Mucilage-slit
In the earth's main cleft.
All grin at the lens,
None at you.
  But me. I watch
From a Tennessee hill
Ten thousand miles off—
You clad in bodies
Raw as eels.
Why ask me to face
Their shame; your modesty,
Your hedged consent?

17. FOR VIVIEN LEIGH

I was the show, reading the murder-suicide
From my novel-in-progress and my heron poem
Whose gaunt last chill mostly rivets the rows
At these odd inexplicable rallies of ears.
(Tonight a radiologist sleeps till peppered
By applause, then bolts up to swear he's heard
Every word—all soothing).
                 At the after-party
I haunt the kitchen, leashing the ego
That—uncurbed now—will howl till dawn.
Slowly the room fills. Again I'm the act,
At a round worktable gnawing tuna and cheese.
A bald man asks me to tell my tale
Of autograph hunting by mail in the 40s.
I run through the early easy successes—
MacArthur in the Phillipines; Eisenhower weaving
The Norman invasion, a shirt of fire;
Toscanini, Barbara Stanwyck on her own stationery
With a skywriting plane inscribing her name
In blue at the top.
              A woman suddenly
Says your name—hadn't I met you?—
And I give them the story that holds them closer
Than my own read-words: the three times in New York,
Stratford, London when you let the black-haired
Boy I was (and am, seeing you)
Come backstage and stand two feet away,
Having kissed your hand, and see, just *see*
Your burning face (we spoke ten minutes
But no word survives).
                  The short years before,
The long years since, no other face moves
In the world yours ceaselessly generates—
Radium lily, slant eyes fixed

On mine (green limpets).
I knew

You were half-mad, knew you were flung
Like a rag real-child off high rock
Walls into real rock gulfs time
After time and rose like this; knew you'd
Blessed me forever—these eyes to thank
In lucid memory each day since:
Perfect, utterly informed, no glint of blame.
   Now a whole new room, twelve still Tennesseans,
   Has watched the gift.

18. SECRET

Any room you entered thirty years ago
Rang for me with the high white pitch
That cows maddogs, guides bats through briars.

Noon today I passed you at St. Patrick's—
You in your old brisk trudge, forcing air;
Jaw still firm—rampart I never took.

I called your name silently, the waves lapped short,
You never broke stride or veered an inch
But pressed on south—home, a new daughter:

One more thing you'll never hear from me.

19. FOR LEONTYNE PRICE (*La Forza del Destino, 1984*)

At the end of the convent scene, act one,
When you'd begged the Virgin to cloak your sin
(In a voice that still might wring quick pardon
From rabid jaws) and were bound for your cave—
Hermit's bell, wretched bread—the abbot handed you
An earnest cross: no toy, nine tall feet
Of staggering wood. You held it upright
A long half-minute as the monks concluded
Their rousing send-off; then you walked it away—
Curtain, cheers.
           I sat still long enough
To fix the sight, knowing I'd seen you
Enact your emblem—ravishing prayer
At shut iron gates, silent assent,
The whole weight borne.

20. CAUGHT

The past three nights were long hot comas,
Requisite maintenance for two jarred weeks
On the road by air. But plainly more.
Beneath the hectic signal of dream
(Last night a fast hour in forced pursuit
Of an old landlady's slick covered trail—
Adulteries bucked-out in wet back alleys),
I know I'm cocked for one right word
That's already flung my way from the source,
Will pass any instant at the speed of black light,
And, lost, will not be beamed again.
   Selfless chemicals I hear toward dawn—
Truth seized and held in juddering eyes,
Final secret of sexual love.

21. CAW

Splayed face-down on the last pool of sleep,
I'm gaffed by *caw-caw* from one distant crow.
What Roman would rise to face this day?

Half an hour later I loom at the pond window,
Glum while my two globes of barnyard cholesterol
Gurgle behind me in salt-free fat

To the tune of the radio voice of Charles Simic
Who suddenly flings out a cold crow poem.
What human would join me to face this day?

22. TRANSATLANTIC

This voice—light-tenor
Ghost of your body—
Hunts me ten thousand miles,
Burns down from its satellite,
And halts me here
(Precisely its laugh)
On the last long step
Into loss of your six smells,
Burr of your neck,
Eyes still by day
As famished stoats
But adrift by night
like well-fed fishers
Borne toward me.

23. A LIFE IN DREAMS

I'm proud second-fiddle today to Eudora's
Seventy-fifth, a sideline smiler, when
A man walks up in the crowded hall—
I met him once, two minutes, years ago
(Classicist, teacher, opera librettist)—
And says he dreamed a new novel by me:
Plot and characters vague but the tone strong as music,
Late Rilke to Schoenberg's *Transfigured Night*;
Each figure guarded and drawn through the maze
By a single angel, gleaming and apt.
He says "I even dreamed the title—
Actual Presences."
                    "Perfect," I say.
"Now write it for me please"; then know I have,
Five times in two decades and mean to again.

24. REST

Day calm and gray as a pewter plate,
Chartreuse new leaves in billows at the glass;
Broody wrens commanding the eaves
With a purpose pure as the laws of ice;

And me—laid-up from the frantic last days
Of a term of students famished as sand,
Winning as fawns (their smoky ordnance
At Milton and God still litters my floor).

Rest. The promise of a week like silt
In a sweetwater delta, stirred only by minnows
And the mutter of each slow skin of nacre
As it welds to the pearl of a somnolent oyster—

Mindless companion while I too mutter
Round my gritty core, this ruined glad life.

25. FOR JAMES DEAN

Twelve months ago we sat here dark,
Apart on the sofa, and watched James Dean
Burn through *East of Eden* like the universal solvent,
Unquenchably craving all bodies, all eyes—
And he underground these twenty-eight years
That silvered my head (two years his junior)
And brought your parents, through whole states of pain,
Together on a late-May bed, starting you.
  We gave him eyes two hours, barely blinking.
The bodies waited another five weeks;
Then fueled by him but balked at the sealed
Dry cleft of his absence, took one another—
Same dark room: a thanks launched deep
Toward his mute head, and running still.

26. THE CLAIM

Since you agreed to live in my house
And sleep like a chloroformed rock through a hundred-
Fifty nights six yards from my hand
(No balks between us), I took this liberty
Throughout your drowned nights; and while I'm still
Unbowed by guilt, I nonetheless feel
At the rim of my mind—like a child's fist tapping
In awe or thirst—this present duty
To full confession, months too late.
 I covered you, every cell of your hide,
With my potent name.
     Potent, I say
Since from age five or six I'd seek lone stretches,
Stare at blank sky, and rattle those thirteen
Letters (three syllables) high and fast
Till they stopped being me and fused into one
Selfless senseless mantra on which I skimmed
More gulfs and peaks in planing light
Than on any other wing—right into pubescence:
That burning air-net, feverish toy.
 You look and see nothing?—follicles, hair,
Moles familiar as dreams of falling
Or maps of home. The sun's too strong.
Stand there in shade by the cleanest mirror.
Gently press the thinnest skin
North of your left eye, bone of your brow.
Step quickly back and focus fine.
See the blood flush in and, for this red instant,
My whole name. Only there on that frail
Supraorbital scrim will it yield to force;
And only there is it boldly legible
As letters, words.
     Elsewhere, from absolute
Crown to sole, you are calligraphed
Invisibly in an endless trail
That is both my name and the framing outline
Of ten thousand pictures, perfect memories

(In universal code of human mime)
Of those two-thousand-two-hundred-fifty minutes
When—merged in mutual angelic maintenance,
Consuming each other like buttered carp—
We earned our vast short seamless luck.
There are scenes in the strongest light on earth
By the deepest sea; scenes in absolute night
By God's hometown, black walls of his house—
You in thriftshop rags and lion head;
Me gimp-kneed, silver, game as you
For the million figures joy can twine
When fearless, fed, and bound to end:
No single mean or ugly turn,
No public sight. You're a shut museum,
No eyes but ours.
                    Caution though—
My lips are sealed; but there's one hard fact
You must bear in mind. My inks are invisible
In normal use—normal pain, daily love.
They'll even hide through quick convulsions
To purge the wells or a conflagration
To clear the scrub. Foxfire however—
Cool constant gleam (blanked by day
But patient to eat whole woods and cliffs)—
Will print you plain as a satellite photo
Of Russian tank-maneuvers toward Texas:
Every tread and finger, thicket and stream.
Any second burn approaching ours
In radiance, stamina, silent roar—
And you'll stand manifest, claimed for life;
Indelible track of the first real name
To vow you all and keep the vow,
Your true best days beneath this hand.

27. TV

At five p.m., grim as Charon's punt,
The neurologist finds me on my stretcher by the door
Of the radiological torture-tank
In which four searchers kind as children
Have found the fault—"A ten-inch tumor
On your spinal cord."
                 Now at nine
I lie here alone, flanked by chatter and howls,
And watch TV—a flabby endless
Documentary, "Portrait of Giselle,"
Starring Anton Dolin with clips of Markova,
Alonso, Makarova: each her own
Absurd self blazed by white elation,
Cause of the helpless joy I sport
In this hot stale proliferating dark.

28. NEIGHBORS

My name is *Edward Reynolds Price,*
So here on the ward I'm *Edward Price.*

Last night I looked at my new neighbor's door.
He's *Edward Reynolds,* plain as ink.

Which one of us is the other's *doppelgänger?*
Scapegoat? Porter of an alternate fate?

29. PEARS

Perfect pears no bigger than hen eggs;
Gold, spotted brown, one mouthful even
For me a boy. My father's brought them
Home from a trip; and I devour
Them in one long evening, then sleep
Black dreamless night till he shakes me—Sunday,
His day.
       Forty-six years pass. Home
From surgery (tumor still in me), I wake
At dawn and taste that cool flesh;
Hear his waking voice.

30. VISION

I'm sleeping with Jesus and his twelve disciples
On the vacant east shore of Lake Kinnereth—
The Sea of Galilee—near where he exorcised
The demon Legion. We're flat on the ground,
Cocooned in clothes. Mine are light street clothes
(Apparently modern, theirs are classic robes);
And I wake early, well before dawn—
Hour of the worm that desolates hope.
I give it long minutes to line another tunnel
With eggs that will yield the next white wave
Of ravenous heirs.
              Then I roll to my right side
And see in the frail dark that Jesus has somehow
Moved nearer toward me. I listen to hear
If he sleeps or wakes.
              Then we stand in the lake,
Both bare to the waist. Light creeps out toward us
From the hills behind; the water's warm.
I see us both as if from a height.
My spine is scored by a twelve-inch incision,
Bracketed now by gentian-purple
Ink that's the map for X-ray therapy
Due in two days. Jesus's beard
Is short and dry, though with both broad hands
He lifts clear water and pours it down
My neck and scar.
              Then we climb toward shore.
I get there first and wait on the stones—
We're still the only two awake.
Behind me he says "Your sins are forgiven."
I think "That's good but not why I came."
I turn and say "Am I also cured?"
He comes close but looks down. He says "That too,"
Then wades strong past me and touches land.

31. THE DREAM OF REFUSAL

I've come on foot through dark dense as fur
(Clean, dry but pressed to my mouth)
To find my mother's father's house
In Macon, N. C. I know he's been dead
Since she was a girl, but—stronger—I know
A secret's here I must face to live.

At the end of seventy miles I see it,
Though the dark's unbroken and no light shows
From any tall window or the open door.
I pull myself through the rooms by hand—
All dead, empty, no stick or thread,
Not the house I loved in childhood

And no more hint of a vital secret
Than noon sun stamps on a working hand.
I forget my life is staked on this hunt,
That these walls store dried acts or words
To kill or save precisely me who pass
Fool-fearless and out again—the yard, lighter dark.

I'm leaving the place and have reached the thicket
Of shrubs near the road. I step through the last
Clear space that can still be called my goal—
My mother's father's home in Macon.
I lift my foot to enter freedom
(And death? I no longer think of death).

Behind me I feel a quick condensation—
Sizable presence barely humming
In furious motion. Fear thrusts up me
Like rammed pack-ice. But I know again
Why I'm here at all, and slowly I turn
Onto whatever deadly shadow waits.

What seems a small man—blackhaired, young—
Crouches in yellow glow he makes,
A smoke from his skin. I know at once
His motion is dance; that he dances every
Instant he breathes, huddled ecstatic.
His hands are empty. He beckons me.

I know he will make his thrust any moment;
I cannot guess what aim it will take.
Then as—appalled—I watch him quiver,
He says "Now you must learn the bat dance."
I know he has struck. It is why I came.
In one long silent step, I refuse and turn toward home.

I will walk all night. I will not die of cancer.
Nothing will make me dance in that dark.

32. OCTOBER SUN

Long silence here—six weeks of days
When numbness climbed my body: this chimney
With ample footholds, a shuddering fire.
But now as dead leaves stroke the house
And crazed squirrels race to hide (from themselves)
The deluge of beech- and hickory-nuts,
I warm again to the heat of life—
A promised stretch of upright time.
The vision of cure in Kinnereth;
The calm white-hot assurance
From six sane friends that I'll survive
In human, useful, usable form
Are credible again.
                              And these words boil up
Sure, unhedged as a year-old boy's
Blue gold-edged eyes.

33. MOTHER

Dear girl, dead twenty years
But hot as new blood,
You're eighty today.

Do you see me here—
Stove-up at fifty-two,
Numb as a plate?

Can you beg for help?
Will your own starved lips
Move once to save me?

34. TURN

Eight months since surgery, six since radiation
(Twenty-seven daily trips to Hiroshima),
I sit in my bedroom, its prisoner,

When my long hope was to hold some other
Inmate, glad to wear my yoke
And smiling not one hand's breadth from my face.

35. LATE VISIT

February 10th, 9:10 a.m.,
Bright icy Sunday—Jeff Anderson phones:
"Look out your window. The heron's on the pond."

Indisputably he is, and frozen out again—
Barred from his breakfast but preening the thousand
Blues of his wings, clearly assuaged.

Seven weeks late for his yearly stop,
Thrown maybe by the crazed local weather
(Coldest month in a hundred years)

Or detained to alter his former message—
Endurance or death. What news today?

THREE

LINES OF LIFE

Various as roads, the lines life takes—
Twisting like the boundaries of lakes.
What we lack here, some god can there increase
With harmonies, amends, enduring peace.

after Friedrich Hölderlin

*Now Joseph, being a man of principle, and not wishing to make
a spectacle of Mary, decided to dismiss her secretly.*

MATTHEW 1:19

THREE SECRETS

1. JOSEPH

That's way too strict a version of the truth.
The principle was—*I'd never seen her like,*
Not in fifty years (and I'd seen a few).
My first wife had died the previous winter;
And once we had her cold underground,
My boys gave skittish signs of dread—
The aged parent, unobligingly hale,
To stuff and josh through centuries more.
Without my knowledge, they set up a hunt—
Some well-fixed widow or crosseyed girl
Who might not gag at stringy hams,
The treacherous tool that let me down
More times than not those last years.
They came back dry and said as much—
"Take it from here; our hands are full."
"—Of the trade I taught you," I thought but didn't say
And turned back to minding my own cot and pots.
Still they'd set me off, and the itch gnawed steady.
So I made my own hunt—dignified, cunning,
Best foot forward—with no better luck;
Then resigned myself to space and peace
(A big, not entirely unwelcome surprise).
Toward spring, however, an old local girl
Moved back up here. She'd married well—
A Temple priest—and lived in the City
Till he keeled over one day, slaughtering doves.
I'd cavorted with her before she got grand
And wondered now what jig was left.

None at all, not a skip—she let me know
On my first visit (and I'd washed my beard).
The daughter though—the blinding girl.
I hardly watched her serving our tea;
My eyes would skid off her face like ice
Or live wood-coals. She looked that rare.
Whatever her mother had had, long since
(Good eyes, straight teeth), whatever the priest—
All boiled in her and changed to skin
Rich as goat's cream, eyes
Deep enough to hold the world.
She never spoke. But as I left
Anne seized my arm and said "Protect her."
I thought she'd gone off her rocker in town;
Baffled, I bowed and scuttled out.
Protect her from what up here?—the odd snake.

But I dreamed about her the next three nights
And then went back to ask Anne's meaning.
She meant what happened, a marriage deal.
And though I faced a hail of jokes,
I kept my bargain and married the girl—
Even with a belly slung on her by then,
A wen gorging hour by hour on blood.

Why? Not principle. Not manly kindness
And—God knew then—not second sight
(The way I saw it, some City boy'd ruined her).
I was glad enough to take people's pity,
Nod my thanks when they said "bighearted."
My heart's big as yours, a small man's fist.

The principle was *her*—all skin and eyes,
Lank horsehair bound at her strong-stalked neck,
The covered promise of undreamed more.

My secret till now (and it scalds to tell)
Is the one fact no one's guessed at yet—
I saw her just once, the whole bare her.
Wracked in dry straw, sweating great clots
Of absolute dread, her bloody thighs
Swung boneless out and blue with agony
To make clear room for that huge head—

Her first live boy, a ten-pound wedge.
The ox-team bent down nearer than I.
　　Years after, back home (the nine years left me),
I never begged more. A younger man
Might have barged through risk to claim that glory—
Even one short night, succeeded by her death.
Not I. I slept at a good arm's length,
Though in reach of her breath—the musk of milk—
Till I died, still stunned.

The angel said to her "The Holy Spirit will come over you, and the Highest Power will darken you." LUKE 1:35

2. MARY

It did, no question.
My hands worked to save me;
The dark was so deep
They couldn't find my body.
My skirt had melted away
In the glare (I felt that much),
And the wind scorched my legs—
The scars are still there,
Though no one's seen them since Bethlehem.
Mother begged to see, any shred
Of proof for the cock-and-bull story
I had to tell—a girl
Flung down by the Last Resort,
His hot seed blown
Into her green womb: a country
Girl, never asked to write
So much as her name, now asked
To gouge it plain enough to read—
An ordinary name in the dome of creation.
    I stood and wrote, apparently
Right—the word still echoes,
A million mouths, each instant
Each year. Who was I, fifteen,
To say flat No?
                Twelve thousand days later—
Toothless, hunched, at his raw
Red feet—I knew my answer
And mouthed it toward him. I doubt
He heard; he was screaming by then.
    So I've held it in, two thousand
Years, and see no cause to speak
It now.

"There are eunuchs who were born that way from their mother's womb. There are eunuchs made eunuchs by men, and there are eunuchs who made themselves eunuchs for the kingdom of heaven." MATTHEW 19:14

3. JESUS

I said as much to test their edge
And waited for the question *Which are you?*
—Sweaty silence. I'd lost them again
To the nearest sight: two amorous dogs
And a peg-legged girl. When would I learn?
I was not meant to be heard but seen,
The final emblem.
                              It was near the end;
I was all but hungry for the final round.
So I let it rest on the humming air
And turned toward blood, thick sheets of blood—
All I had.
                    The question waits though,
Three-pronged riddle any man must solve
For himself or choke—*Who cut my roots?*
The lines to power, and why, and so what?
My premise plainly was *Power is flesh.*
Man's power—woman's—maybe God's,
Flesh as it yokes with alien flesh
In single relays, bearing the charge
Till flesh burns out and is someway replaced.
   Me? I came here fully equipped,
All requisite organs, members, glands;
All ticking dimly at the human rate—
A fresh bud here, a wilting there,
Crisp hair and eighteen separate scents:
All triggered also by natural time.
At fourteen no boy anywhere near me
(Where we swam in the quarry) showed more than I—
A convex exhibit of Ready Boy,
The height of the climb, my splendid noon.

All wasted, unspent? All slashed and hurled
In the rank dog's-bowl?
                    Never, no.
The loyal women who watched me nailed,
Hung high to drip, know I died intact—
A youngish man still fit to stamp
His face on countless scores of souls
As yet blank, dumb, in the waiting line.
Even soldiers flung up cheers
At my pelvic gear.
                    So yes, I chose;
It was not specified in my commission.
I made myself this dead-end road
I walked to the end, this low Skull Hill.
I vowed it at twelve when my fork took life,
And twenty-one years I kept the vow
With no more ease than a healthy stallion
Tethered in a field of fragrant mares.
More nights and dawns than any friend knew,
I gnawed the heel of my hard right hand
To purple pulp to balk my yen
To know the common sweetness of skin.
  Why? I knew I'd need clear gaze,
No flickering others at the rim of sight,
No colored glass between me and day.
I was the prism, sole translator
Of this whole world that poured through me
Toward God's own mind—the stroke of dark,
Light, jackal-crunch of teeth in bone,
Human eyes so swamped by pain
I'd have howled and run except for the choice.
Every conscious moment, I stopped my arm
On the near edge of touch. Healing, scourging,
Anointing, yes; never the melding
That brings frank joy, knowledge and joy—
Likewise shackles, blinders, gags.
  That was the cost. *I was always free.*
I could speak any syllable that creased my mind

(No family glares)—sleep in the dirt
Where I happened to tire—raise a cold corpse
Without its permission and then walk out.
Few ever saw me twice, except the twelve pupils.
They were close-by daily, huddled close at night;
But they were who I touched least of all—
Once when I tapped them to follow me;
Second, that last time as they sat bolting
Down broiled perch to numb their betrayal
And I stepped through the shut door—live!
They had to touch me to prove their fear.

He meant all he said. This country eunuch
With a two-edged tongue, a babymaker
In mint condition (never unwrapped),
This silvery bore died in the pain
That splits black granite in the hearts of hills
And stands here now, skin pierced but closing—
Reach here in the side, know a new brand of flesh.

I managed, just, to bear their touch—
One by one, eleven in line;
And then the three women, diehard loyals
From the earliest days. I thought I'd shrink,
That the flesh itself would flee their hands
As it always had.
                            But no, it held
In place for all three (Magdalen last).
And as they rushed out to scrounge me a bowl,
Salvage some scraps—I must be starved—
I suddenly saw a changed new world,
Sight strange to me as my face to this room,
What my vow had forbade my knowing till now.
Each particle linked, perpetual chain:
Yoking, binding, bonding in glee
These fourteen before me, old companions,
Now newly born, more welcome than rain—
Bumping and jostling to dry my hair,
Guiding my elbow on to the bench
They'd cleared to bear me, crouching round,
Hand joined to hand at the white core of space

Where they'd been from the start,
The lovely tread of lean and hold
—Which I knew in an instant I now must flee.
I wept hot tears to learn so late.

ROAD

Dead vine on dead tree, evening light, one crow,
Low bridge, streaming water, empty house,
Old road (the Road), cold wind, a starving horse.
Sun falls on broken man at edge of day.

after Ma Chih Yuan

THREE VISITS

1. DIONYSOS

A god stopped in at the house last night,
Claiming to be a Jehovah's Witness
Peddling tracts and offering to expound
John's Apocalypse—what it meant for me.
   I pierced his mask at once—two mistakes.
I lied at the door and claimed to be Catholic
(A claim that always halts true Witnesses);
But he never flinched so I let him in,
Asked him to sit, and awaited his purpose.
Then as he bent to sip a cup of water
(All he'd accept from my profuse bar),
I saw a two-inch edge of leopard skin
Otherwise hid by his white Arrow shirt—
Hot and spotted at his tawny neck,
The formal dress of Semele's son.
   We bumbled through numb amenities—
The glorious day, rags of a staggering
Fall aurora north of my door
(He took clear family pride in that).
I felt we were warming, felt I'd won his trust,
That now we'd surely proceed to his secret
On some straight beneficial path.
And his next few gambits seemed propitious—
What did I feel about his eyes?
Did he have some major unfilled need?—
   But once he'd drained the glass, he dozed—
Lounging slack in the deep plush chair,
Gold eyes blank as aluminum washers,
The short dense body melting till it formed
A lithe live-model of the seat and arms,
The finest slipcover this side Elysium.
The transformation took ten minutes

But felt like a geologic era—
A casual dozen million years.
   Watching it from my new wheelchair
(The first improvement in invalid gear
Since the Crimean War), I helplessly underwent
Conversion—conforming like liquid to my seat
And wheels, agreeing to this crouched rolling
Life as endless, my mere fate
On earth and under, a likable mode.
Poured out, dumb, we both lay on
Just past an hour (my digital watch
Chimed cheerful eight and his hide shuddered).
   Then slowly still his essence gathered;
Limbs, trunk, head throbbed, coalesced—
A second prolonged transformation.
The glare consumed his peddler's mask
Till he sat up near my face, then rose—
Himself revealed, incendiary core,
A megatonnage unforeseen
By any computer or institute:
Precisely the grandest male I'd found,
Exhaling from every pore of a skin
Dusted with a pelt of slant tan hair
The constant ground-bass of majesty.
   Scared, I hunkered through the long bombardment,
Guessing I'd scorch to a charcoal crackling
Like his dimwit mother in the throes of Zeus.
I didn't, though I heard my eyebrows singe.
Eventually I could nod and I spoke his name—
Syllabic thunder, in school-Greek.
It must have been the test; I passed.
   His right arm moved out toward me then;
In its field of force, I also grew—
Firmed and steadied till I rose to meet him,
Irresistibly drawn onto legs
Again as apt as a working boy's
In a field of furrows of standing grain:
Not the filleted flippers I've lately worn.
   Then entered me—the god himself.

Or I entered him (it was all his plan,
I knew, his purpose). Either way we melded
Through the next calm epoch into one discrete
Bounded body of a grace and spangle
I'd only guessed in pornographic moments
Of boyhood, rapt at Father's fogged pierglass—
I devouring gouts of his power,
Undying springs of riot and calm;
He absorbing my new skill,
Invented, patented by mortal man
(The means of thriving on a void salt prairie,
At the entire mercy of all that moves
On foot, segmented belly, or wing:
Gnats, chilled vipers, the odd escaped arsonist
Or neighbor-punk with knucks and shiv).
    Then separated, again slowly as leaves eat light.
What he was by then assisted me back
Cross the steerhide rug to my patient chair
Which seemed, in his hands, tolerable home.
Silent, he brought me cool tapwater
In the cup he'd drunk from (my good silver).
As I bent to sip, he gripped my skull
In a force I knew was bound to kill
(Calmest thought of the past two years).
But then relented; met my eyes
A final time with his (not blank now,
Plunging slow through infinite mind);
And left the way he'd come—off east
Up Cornwallis Road toward the upright, town:
The shifting lights of the crazed-for-motion,
Jolt of willed contingency.
    Whoever else detected him
On his gleaming way, I've yet to hear—
Outrage or praise, death-rattle or glee.
    I even wondered most of the night
At my own answer—rage or thanks?—
Till dawn when I woke in the same brass bed
I can no longer roll in and rolled my tongue
On the tart astringence of early grapes,

Then raised and saw my sensible threatened
Working arms woven in tender
Young green vines: tendrils reaching
Toward my heart,
                Which pines for touch.

2. APHRODITE

The spring I was fourteen we lived in a house
That had been a recent massacre-scene,
Greek in volume—a Mr. Young
Locked himself and his wife in a bedroom
And beat her hard. A grown son pounded
The door in rescue. The father fired
Through the wood, killed the son;
Then killed the wife and, neatly, himself.

    When we moved in, the door was patched
With plastic wood; but the sheetrock ceiling
Bore two neat holes (superfluous shots).
My family'd never known the Youngs.
Still we kept the scene as our spare bedroom;
And Mother thumped my younger brother
When he'd tell guests they had the "Bullet Room."

    I conspired in the secret but kept the room
As a sulking chamber for afternoon pouts
(I was crawling, appalled, through my own hail—
A puberty stern as trench warfare
With poison gas).

                One Sunday in June
I shut myself in and turned the key—
Ferocious self-service succeeded by a doze
And scraps of stolen satiate dream.
When I woke sun was broiling the blinds
In orange fire; and a full-grown woman
Stood by the bed, naked as any
Forced magnolia—that white, flamboyant,
Stupifyingly rank.

              The face was nearly
My mother's—familiar in humming vibrance—
But the hair was long and bound at the neck
With amber pins, a few strays gleaming;
And the belly bore no scar like Mother's
(Aftermath of a burst appendix).
Elsewhere she managed to cantilever
A magnanimity of flesh that poised

On the razor-edge of corpulence—
An endless clearly magical No
To gravity and its train of bylaws.
    I'd dreamed such luck for three, four years
And pictured it frankly in my locked diary.
This was plainly no dream—dreams flaunt no odor—
And when my left hand stretched to try her,
The hair in her fork was sufficiently charged
To halt a herd of yearling bulls.
I drew back, burned, and sucked my finger.
    She smiled, begged pardon—"I always forget"—
Stood a moment to damp her voltage,
Then folded in pliant glory beside me.
    I'd known so little joy till then
(All solitary, all mainly outdoors—
Childish transports, though truer than adult
Beatific unions with angel thighs,
Cherubic darts pumping flame),
I froze in blue paralysis,
Cowlick to crotch, and expected death.
No Methodist boy could butt through this
Not stamped on the brow with a black-scabbed *L*
For goatish lust, passport to the Pit.
    She understood, stroked my rigid belly,
And murmured a word I heard as *Cyprus*.
    I'd finished the eighth grade, studied myths,
And understood she'd named her birthplace—
The sea off Cyprus, wind-blown foam,
Pregnant scallop-crib of ardor.
The knowledge freed me. I grinned wide as Kansas,
And blood crept out from my clenched heart
To my locked limbs, chiefly my third leg
(The sturdy friend that'd seen me through).
But I knew no way to enact the force
Beyond the handy grip of palms,
The knowing permanent portable socket
I'd found ten years ago and trained
To the fleet dispatch of consoling perfection.
    She seized control and in the next hour—

To muffled sounds behind the patched door
(Father's day-off shuffle, my brother at the keyboard
Hellbent to bang out *Adeste Fidelis*
In the Bombay-day)—she endowed on me
A Himalayan glide toward snow-saddled heights
Of corporal joy I accepted with helpless
Copious tears of dumb amazement
And the inexhaustible readiness of boyhood
But also the certainty that never, with no one
Less than she in the maybe sixty years
That lay before me, would I stride so high
On so bright a ridge in blinding light
That deigned not to blind but aimed my eyes
To a piercing keenness that laid back skin
And peeled the ample spine of pleasure
That waits unimplorable, unforeseen
In the will of God, gods, their hapless consorts.
    Both ways I was right—I made the climb,
I bear the scars (concealed red stripes,
Authentic as the oozing wounds of Francis),
I've sought their mate in a hundred bodies:
All lovely, most human, some demi-divine
(She'd left when I roused from a ten-second stun;
The house was more than naturally still,
Dozing in its own grateful lustration).
    No subsequent match (though a few proximations
For which I burn the lamp of thanks);
So I live as the human—only one I know—
Who flowered on the low near-sill of life:
Young as a Rebel drummer at Shiloh,
Now an aging vet, grateful, grinning
And fueled by hope of a second bloom
But privately hunched for the downhill path
Torched by memory, dimming daily.

3. HERMES PSYCHOPOMPOS

Sit with me, utterly still at dusk. Look there
To the left of the big beechtree (always askance;
He's prevented or shied by a direct stare—more than glances,
Flicks at scraps of his face). Hold still; the hour
Of the hawk's at hand.
                                        There, sweeping toward us cross
The field—the redtailed hawk who rules
The beech (though daily contested by wrens). There,
It's seized the roosting bough at the crotch of the trunk;
It knows we're here but conserves its grandeur, the iron
Eyes by a pure disdain that all but deletes us.
    The sky falls now, light years per instant. In four
More seconds he'll take his place—the man in question
(If he's on tonight; three nights each lunar month
He's off, though I've yet to succeed in cracking his code,
Whatever schedule dictates the vigil.
                                        Now. *There*—
Cut an eye quick to the low leafpile: his bare
Feet (no, no heel wings). Now up the runner's legs,
Long waist, strong neck to the wide gray eyes—
Lucid gray of frozen dawn and locked
On me from here till sleep. Enough. Rest.
    That—in jeans and chambray workshirt—is almost
Surely the high gods' messenger, guide of souls
Through death to life (whatever life waits, there
On the extreme verge of breath—recompense,
Tonic lines of the fugue we'll play till time resolves,
Or near-starvation like Odysseus' mother when he finds
Her in Hades—so desperate she laps hot blood from a ditch
When her son dispatches a ram to save her). *Hermes
Psychopompos* there in my yard where
He's waited more than twenty years—for who else
But me, sole resident?
                                        First he came
As a string of beasts, all but perfectly transformed
Scouts—a great blue heron recurring each Christmas,
A more than normally watchful redfox,

A small herd of three unflappable deer
At my study window, a pale uncanny near-fetal
Cat that stalked my terrace the day Mother died
And one more day years later when I sat
Laughing with two friends, recalling the cat; and there
It was on the windowledge pressed to the pane
Intent on me (both witnesses are live, sane, ready
To testify); possibly a very peculiar blacksnake,
Also recurrent and able to speak.
       But human,
In that form there tonight—he's only come thus
Since the day I finished five weeks' radiation
(Twenty-nine thirty-second trips to Hiroshima, ground-zero,
Blast). At first I thought it was my new neighbor;
Then a peeping Tom (sorry, no flasher). Then
As the held-off astonished baked nerves in my spinal cord
Began to die (they never revive in human
Tissue) and my hips and legs became boiled noodles,
Then wet rags, I'd search his evening manifestations
For some plain sign he was more than he seemed.
         I never
Found more than what's there now, by the beech before us—
A young man barefoot in all grades of swelter, rain,
And ice; black-haired, gray-eyed, low-browed: he never
Looks down but locks on my face fiercely
As a satellite circling Russia on a missile-
Hunt through frozen tundra and sleepless armies
Of golden elk or clouds of gray geese steered
By the moon, magnets buried in the thrumming earth,
And patterned stars.
      Soon he'll face me and bear
My gaze. Then you'll know I've named him right.
He's come for me. Or waits. He flies no sign
Of impatience, though it's more than a year
And though I've strengthened nicely again—
From waist to brain.
       Is he Hermes then in another
Aspect?—god of fraud, deceit, good luck,
God of dice, wealth, body games? Am I soon

To be the first gimp billionaire, first gimp wheeler
Of a four-minute mile, first wheelchair-spy (compromising
Star Wars and avoiding jail as a privileged minority)?
    Is he Hermes at all or, more, Apollo—god
Of healing, light, streaming music? Apollo, dark,
Enduring nights in a Tarheel winter, iced limbs
Crashing round his head till day, famished squirrels
Gnawing his toes?
                  Hermes surely. Should I call him
In? Roll out to meet him, ask for his papers,
Offer him cocoa, the evening news?
                            I jest. I know.
I've seen his staff. Notice there at the base
Of the tree—the peeled stick propped and bound with what
Seem vines or rope? They're two dark serpents, often
Live but rigid now, though I've watched them writhe.
He granted me that much the night he first arrived
As himself (or his familiar guise). When my eyes caught
Him standing, he gravely brandished the staff
Before him; serpents both faced me and writhed.
(The best texts claim they were given Hermes by Lord
Apollo who'd sanctified the snake to healing
Because of its gift of renovation—its trick
Of shedding last year's skin, even the surface
Cells of eyes. Snakes though were also sacred
To Pluto, god of death, for the pure efficiency
Of venom and grip.)
                So. I'm finally resolved
To stand. Or sit, awaiting his patient will.
He's all but too fine to stay there posted behind
Thick glass; but calling him in would force his hand—
Entire healing (new life, erect) or condescension
(The broad initial step to entire dark and death).
    Not after all, the first god—gorgeous as life
And death—I've left outside in night and rain,
Though he offered care.

YOUR BLOOD

You boast of your day's freedom, wisdom, mercy
And call the times before you wild and dark.
They crawled at least through torture, murder, dread;
Through grimace, error, frenzy to a god.
The first crime of your age was—kill the god,
Hack out an idol nothing like His face,
Pet him with names gruesome as no other's;
And fling the best you have, meat for his jaws.
You call it *our* way and will not stand calm,
Racing in drunken fury till—alike,
Cowards and vendors—not red blood of God
But idol's pus gutters through your veins.

after Stefan George

HELIX

This dense lactescence—pattern to repeat
The blank unprecedented fact of you
(Smallest gasping valve that drains a heart,
Southward arc of coarse hair down a brow,
Cheerful jack to pump the spiral plan)—
Is uncracked cipher, flung to waste on me?
   Pause at its drying glaze across my eyes,
Tongue still ruminating its command;
Consider thick potential tribes of children—
Astonished, feeble hands slack at blue thighs—
Hanging in belly-dark for one white word
To strengthen, stride, gesticulate in light:
Deeds of kindness, poems of fate and grace.
   Thrust again. Endow these endless heirs.

I AM TRANSMUTING

I am transmuting. Since you touch my heart,
It gilds inside me. Look, I turn to gold.
Stone I carve, plaster that I paint
Assumes new worth—warnings, praises, glories.
So since your face scored target on my eyes
And I still live, pocked by your barrage,
I move in armor, forged by incantation;
Halt for nothing, nothing harms me now.
I walk on water, walk unscorched through flame;
I kindle light in beggars blind from birth,
And my warm spit sucks poison from hot sores.

after Michelangelo Buonarotti

A TOMB FOR WILL PRICE

A serious visit demands at least three hours of your life,
Preferably starting on a summer evening and stretching till dark
When you're shown the secret. Any quicker tour will deny you the secret,
And no initiate is permitted to tell you. Applications are
Made in personal script, with two unaltered recent
Photographs, to me as guide. I choose and respond the day
Received with either the stiff white dated ticket—no fee
Is charged—or courteous refusal, no explanation.

You come alone a little past seven, clear high evening,
Crisp new moon declaring herself on the hip of the sky.
I meet you at the gate, offer you water from the ordinary fountain
With a worn foot-pedal, indicate the shed half-banked in holly
(Your only toilet). Then while I walk you on toward the mouth,
I recite the few facts you can use to start; the rest are comprehensible
Only inside, in the ultimate light—
    "The rooms preserve and honor the builder's memory
Of his father's life in eastern and piedmont North Carolina.
The builder is I, his elder son (no surviving daughters)—
Sole builder. I've had nor wanted no other help.
The aim is to guide you back through the life, to a sense of its actual
Weight and refraction, the consequence of an actual quest
For radiant virtue by a traveling salesman of freezers and stoves.
It's all underground, dug out by hand—my hands, as I said—
And braced with beams. It may never be finished. We can enter now."

The first room's largest and entirely finished; it contains the museum—
Based on the old brand of roadside farrago he could never resist:
Some aging rattletrap's cases of bird eggs, blown and mislabeled;
Some veteran Rough Rider's curling postcards of Cuban canebrakes
And veiled señoritas, a lock of black hair bound with red twine,
And a withered arm still hung on the vet, a hook for a hand.
I display only relics of his life before me, my ill-timed birth
At his lowest ebb. Amazingly few were found to survive;

Our gypsy years had deleted his youth—only this pair
Of *pince nez* glasses I never saw him wear, copied from his idol,
Woodrow Wilson; an autographed letter from Wilson himself
Thanking my father (nineteen years old) for his manly support
Of the threatened League; the fossilized bones of a fried-chicken dinner
His mother cooked him to eat on the train toward National Guard
Camp in Morehead City; the pink invoice for a string
Of pearls he gave my mother at their engagement; the box
Of talcum in which he stored a single birthcontrol
Device in Depression years when penury ruled even boyish
Lust; a travel diary with his sales reports for 1929
(Penniless year); a letter from the pastor who dredged him howling
Through alcoholism; the draft of a poem to greet his first child,
Should she prove a daughter: "*Loved long before your eyes appeared,
I love you more now you lie in my hand.*"

                                        Second, an unfinished
Replica of the space he was born in—a dim attic dormer, barely
Headroom to stand. If I last, I'll hunt out the deep brown bed,
The stained mezzotint of "A Shepherd's Kiss," the actual air
He recalled till his death—gold light, dust motes, the salt scent
Of blood. His mother's hair, two chestnut strands coiled loose
On the pillow. His father's revolver—clean, loaded—on the mantel.
All exist somewhere; no matter is lost. I must simply hunt.
The atoms spin at our ears this instant, yearning to converge
In their old shapes—the forms they filled to cradle him.
Pause here to listen, a wiry cry at the threshold of sound.
I watch to see if you truly hear. You plainly do.

   Now we are dark. Night falls at our feet. So I read the prelude
To mystery, my final disclosure. *Next room, the secret—
Core of the tomb and demonstration of all he meant.
Expect no danger, no threat to your eyes. Only the fact
His quest discovered, opulent bloom on the utmost branch
Of the single limb he managed to grow in fifty-four years.
Move in silence one step behind me, hand on my shoulder.
I turn the key. Open your eyes.*

                        The man before you
In the overstuffed chair is no real man but a risen body.
It passed through agonized life and death in the common way

A Tomb for Will Price

And is now changed flesh, changed bone and hair. My dedication,
Your need to see, have earned it leave to come back here
And wait for you—proof of the soul, perpetual life;
Risen flesh in the form it will hold till all time ends.
Note the eyeglasses, apparent bifocals, thin gold frames—
The eyes behind them, clear steel-gray; the speckled hands
Mottled with age. Note the wide lips, parted to speak,
Moist with yearning to call your name. No words come;
He's lost your language, knows only the nine chief angel tongues
Unknown on earth. Even I'm unable to hear his message.
But look, he'll smile. He's resigned to smile, his one plain message.
It aims at you. Nod your acceptance. You may touch him once—
I suggest the right cheek, flushed with strength.
                                        Now he'll sleep upright;
The visits tire him; he requires long rest. In his sleep a music
Spins at the crown of his head. We won't stay to hear.

Finished. You're free. Find the long way home; hold the secret safe.
It may not be conveyed, as I warned—can't be. Urge friends and kin
To come on their own; it must be their choice, their need and courage.
I'll greet and serve them as I've served you, in simple joy.
Urge them to hurry; I've strained to my limit and may not last—
No guarantee of the sight if I fail. No heir to my work
If I cannot finish. No servant to tend this eternal father.
Will a soul at the white-heat need my tending, miss my presence?
I can only affirm he has never faced me, never smiled toward me
As toward all others.
                    Ignore my fears, they are my last secret;
A burden I never foresaw but must take (what burden's foreseen)?
Say only, I offer the sole exhibit on this earth now of the final
Hunger—a visible soul.
                    As you leave, climb slowly. The path's
Lit only by your new light. You may not return.

MIDNIGHT

At midnight, half-unwilling, I would walk—
A boy, lonely boy—past that churchyard,
Past Father's house, the pastor's; star on star,
Each separate, burned beautiful and clear
  At midnight.

Then when later in my distant life
I ran to meet my darling where she lay,
Stars and aurora struggled overhead—
I going, coming, breathing happiness—
  At midnight.

Until at last the full moon's radiance
Pierced my darkness cleanly, absolutely;
And my mind—willing, knowing—rushed to twine
With past and future waiting where they lay
  At midnight.

                      after Johann Wolfgang von Goethe

HOUSE SNAKE

All summer it seemed a fair exchange—
Black snake on the lot, better mouser
Than a cat (the previous winter I'd lost
Eighty pages of Marcus Aurelius and a Phaidon
Michelangelo to squads of mouse teeth).
He could prowl the crawl space
Round furnace and pump, have whatever
Life was separate from me—frogs,
Baby birds, chipmunks, scuttling mice,
The chance copperhead wandered up
From the pond. I'd receive the service
Of his plunder and pay only rarely
In frigid instants of seeing him—
Breakfasting, sapped by bliss, on the porch;
Turned by the chime of a silent signal
To find him embossed on the beechtree
Above me, string of hot tar
Ready to pour (*does he see me?*)
Or thrust down, rigid as a cane,
From the gutter, devouring raw wren-
Hatchlings in the house I'd suspended on wire
To miss his reach.
              I learned to take
That much—and with measured pride:
One of my early templates was Mowgli,
An agreeably imitable brunet boy
Whom large beasts loved or anyhow
Addressed in lucid warnings and thanks
For service; so his tolerance in admitting
My presence was a parched hard honor
I mentioned to no one, though aloud
I thanked him one late August morning
As he elevated his bullet head
And ten inches of neck from unmown

Grass at the utmost limit of the neutral
Zone where fear began—mine
And his, I'd thought; the line of our agreement,
Real on the ground as a chain of voltage.
I watched him, still as he; then smeared
A palm on intervening air,
Set down my coffee, and said "Thanks,
Nero"—naming him as Adam
Named the stock of Eden, spontaneously,
Straight homage to his essence: clandestine, pure
Black. I turned to eat again and by
The time I remembered him, he'd soundlessly dissolved.
That afternoon I needed a book
From the dining room (semi-basement,
Drowned in must). I was wearing shorts
And no form of shoes; the room was shuttered,
Slotted dark. I was down—six feet
Toward the dimmest core—before a voice,
Clear as airport advice, said
"You should have worn shoes this far
Underground." I stopped, midstride,
And solicited my feet. It took a long
Moment for eyes to gape the stagnant
Murk—two beige feet, flat
As buckwheat cakes (apparently mine)
And one crooked yard of black snake
Watching, a step to the right.
Nijinsky at his zenith never equaled
The leap I launched on the instant.
I swallowed a lobe of my heart, sorted
Options—fetch the shovel, chop him up
(And the rug) or pin his head, lift him;
And restore him to his beat, his larger half
Of the premises: nature. He made no feint
As I padded to the stairs, seized the stout-
Handled broom, and (ignoring my bare legs)
Descended to snare him—every nerve by now
Worming through my pores to cling aghast
To the upright hairs of neck, arms, calves.

He'd waited, so still that—a light switched on—
I wondered for the first time if he might
Be dead. He was not merely flat
From nose to tail but deflated,
Merging with the rug, seeping down.
I extended the blond broomstick,
Brushed his neck.
     Ignition.
He flung two-thirds of his length up and back,
Parabolic stake in the new
Usurpation, and defied my intent.
Frozen at the marrow, I at once took
The dare and thrust the first stroke
For my demesne—floor, walls, roof;
Hope of unscathed nights, companioned
By my own taste in guests. *I'll take him;*
Expel him, alive and whole, to the zone
Conceded.
    He fenced, live leather,
Through dazzling changes—hydra, basilisk,
Devouring rod.
     I steadily assured
Myself he was harmless—baby-
Teeth and no venom sacs—as I
Parried his lunges, resplendent in power
And perfect in aim: strike after strike
He gummed the broomstick, sparing me
(I assumed I was spared).
       After maybe two
Minutes of torrid duel, he betrayed
Exhaustion—a shudder at the pitch of his grandiose
Lash. In thirty more seconds,
I pressed him to the rug and, before I could climb
A new rung of fear, bent
And firmly clamped his neck in thumb
And forefinger. I paused for his answer,
More than half-expecting a last transformation
To steal him from me;
      but he

Bore our juncture, my victory,
Pressing on me nothing worse than skin
With the dry packed vigor of slate.
He was straight as Aaron's magic staff,
Unmoving.
        So in that clutch, poised
Between grip and strangulation, I rose;
He streamed down viscid from my fist;
I stepped toward the yard door—
One, two strides.
        He threw
A lightning coil round my wrist;
Then as I halted, astonished, threw
Bracelets toward the hinge of my arm,
His whole present self consumed
In the work. Constriction began—uniform
Clasp of a bloodpressure sleeve
Pumped toward implosion.
        I knew he could **do**
No serious harm; but stalled at the door,
I thought of one sure way
To shed him—chop my arm off.
We moved into tons of sunlight,
I at least glad to be back in his
Place. At the edge of trees, I raised
My captive-capturing hand and faced
His face—no face: machined
Consumers of sight, smell, prey.
The black tongue stroked at air
For my plan—death or release. I
Asked him his. No more answer from **that**
Ensemble of obsidian curves and plates
Than from my own species at similar bay.
But I knew a way out. Had he thrilled
That toward me through thickening light?—light
Was stacking round us, too humid
To speed.
        With my left hand I took
The blunt tip-end of his tail

From my right armpit and, holding
The garlanded arm out—caduceus!—
From my body, I slowly untwined in broad
Safe loops. He barely resisted.
When I had him (straight as he'd ever been)
Before me, I extended him westward;
Then realized I'd generated one more
Vatic pose—hierophant
In some unmanageable rain-forest,
Placating night as it eats another
Day. I'd seen a last problem—
How to set him down. If I dropped him at my feet,
He could launch a final bite. With arms
Still out and up, his undulance between
Them, I threw him broadside.
                  He landed
In undergrowth three steps beyond,
Calm gelid *S*, monogram
Of something. He was not watching me
Or the walls of my house nor was he fleeing;
And only a hardened anthropomorphist
Could entertain the thought that he thought of me;
Remembered me even now, a moment
Apart.
         I reminded him "Out *here*."
If the sounds ever reached him,
He didn't budge. I turned
And went in, lit the downstairs
Room to stadium brilliance, and searched
The floor—clean as a surgical scrub-brush,
No cast skin, no tail. I headed
For the sink and scoured my own hide;
And within half an hour was mostly
My self, altered only by the burr
Of one new fact—*He knows*
The way in, a secret
Way. The whole next morning
I roamed my perimeters, chinking holes,
Blocking grills; and for two weeks

After, I never saw him once—
Though the number of times I told the tale
Of our congregation might have lured the shyest
Monster back for a second go
At the battle bard.
                Then an ordinary night
(Nearer four a.m., heat a steady
Hand at my mouth), I woke on my back,
Aware of company. Dazed, I shuffled
Candidates—visitors longed-for, two
Or three dreaded. I turned my head
Right and kissed the spare pillow, cool,
Unburdened. My arms swept slow half-
Circles at my sides, unrewarded.
I was three-fourths gone again before my left
Hand on its own recognizance slid
From the one sheet and scouted my chest,
Belly, thighs, groin—usual
Automatic meaningless tumescence,
Concomitant of dreams erotic as knitting.
Below the compact bulse of scrotum,
Fingers encountered another coiled
Mass that—stroked on the grain—was fishskin
Rough and remarkably cool in the ambient
Swelter. I suspected it was he; no fear
Arrived, fast or slow. I was somehow
Resigned or, truer, curious.
                He apparently
Reciprocated. A minute to read the coded
Data of my sluggish blood; then he calmly
Rose through unresisting hands
(My right hand had joined him); through
Genitals, belly, breast to my neck.
My hands trailed his abandoned wake
Of body that seemed more an odor
Than palpable presence, rank not putrid—
Another staked claim to be
Here, safe. His tongue lapped
The stubble point of my chin, fed

There by whatever mineral scurf or exhalation
He'd hunted out. My hands felt
Wrenching swallows down his sides—
A nourishment urgent as the wolf-found
Boy's, drunk on death, and slow
As the parting of tectonic plates—
But he didn't grow. Some poised stasis
Was eventually achieved, entire annexation
In which I concurred. I assumed he rested,
Converting what he'd skimmed off me
Into the strength he needed most.
I frisked my body for depredation
And found no change—same moderately well-
Formed limbs, going slack (no fault
Of his). In hopes of guessing his purpose
Here, I searched his length again—firm
As old bread but warmer, stiller:
No rigor of anger, vengeance, or famine
(Benevolent incubus—succubus—both),
And no detectable tick of intent.
So I lay suspended in active patience—
Tired but not fearful so much as alert,
Passively watchful like any gripped creature
And fending off rags and flares of dream,
The traps onto sleep.
     He spoke at last
Or managed to speak; had he tried from the start?
Had our transaction awarded him power
To say his piece? There was nothing a monitoring
Instrument could have caught; yet I heard it as voice—
The lean andante clarification
Native to youthful baritone humans
But flat inhuman, like nothing born
Of woman since the picnic grounds of the Olduvai
Gorge were discontinued. His head
Was somewhere below my left ear,
Not touching skin. His tail still
Looped at evident random in my now-
Cool groin where my right thumb

Flicked the free rim of scales;
So the voice may have transpired by bone
Osmosis—an uncanny sympathy
Of all-night companions, however
Bizarre. I affirm this true report:
"They watch you with interest
After so many years.
One of us has sampled
You at least each year
For the hours prescribed
Of sleep and day,
Employing the usual
Sounding procedures;
Instructed till now
To avoid detection.
I alone failed
But, since you spared me,
Am sent back
On sufferance
To meet your mercy
With payment rendered—
The essence we know,
Having known you entirely
(Your private titles,
Precise destination,
Balance to date).
I require permission,
However; you are free
To refuse receipt."
                    I at once
Refused—who would bear his sentence an instant
Early or from any mouth but the Certified
Horse's Himself, enraged, and attended
By seraphs congested with ire, not a renegade
Egg-thief's, terror of wrens? And of all
Things, I dozed then, drugged
On awe.
          Dawn—rare work-bound
Cars on the road, my own mouth slimed—

I woke alone. Hands affirmed
His absence; eyes gauged the room.
Unaltered, spared—all but memory,
Me. I replayed the theophany in fine
Particular; and while I again weighed
The chance that what I'd endured was retrograde
Delusion (legacy of childhood days
Bogged in Poe), the certainty of earnest
Visitation outweighed. I'd balked at revelation.
Who else in the record of Israel and Christendom
Had flat said No to a visible, audible,
Graspable deputy of Central Wisdom
With news at his lips?—my secret name,
Point of my life, debit or gain.
First I bathed (no punitive scouring now);
Then searched the house—nothing—
Then chose a slow breakfast on the porch
As my sign of regret and proffered submission.
A ragged parade of other beasts passed—
Spiders drugged with expectance, strolling ants;
Sixty feet downhill, the spinster muskrat
Endlessly nesting in the pond's clay dam
For broods that methodically decline to appear,
An obese cock-robin of startling eloquence—
Till I'd also sunk in dumb blind patience.
There.
            Two yards northeast of my seat,
Conformed to white creek-rocks in the ditch,
He'd materialized (how long ago?)—
Right eye toward me. I wiped
One hand, slow, between us in air
Much cooler than the night. I said "Permission."
He moved—or managed to advance two lengths
From rocks to ground (I saw no motion,
Only registered change). On the brilliant moss
Of my acid soil, he was his precise
Self again—common yard-dragon,
Wholly unearthly. I sat, assuming he
Posed for me (his head was barely

Up, immobile; no sign of the tongue).
Then I saw beyond him a condensed brown
Toad, appalled in his glare. The three of us
Froze—a garden-group, mixed media;
"Permutations of the Hunt." Toad and I
Had mutely yielded to what seemed
A hunger ferocious as dwarf stars'—
The bungholes of space, cold ravening.
It would not take us.

                  Never turning to me
Again, he broke his stare at the toad; dropped
His head through minute fractions of space,
Joined the ground in all his length, and moved—
Hauling on through dead leaves, the spindly azalea,
With languid sidelong flings of the spine
Till I'd lost his wake.

                  The toad gave no sigh
Of gratitude, relief, only kept its place
With the ponderous contentment that implies complicity.
Had my refusal of the daunting message
Demoted the messenger to predator now?
Had I been his chance at ascent on any
Ladder he climbed? I rose to find him;
The toad flinched (a heartening proof
Of my weight). He'd left no discernible trail
Or trace—not even the customary belly-
Sweeps of a doomed ground-dweller.
On the chill face of evidence, I could
Say he vanished a handspan beyond
The desolate peachtree I'd planted years
Before that failed to thrive—it stood on
Gamely, limber as a buggy whip, one lateral
Branch with six tender leaves
And the thickening knuckles of premature age.
Even there, in real sun, I clearly thought
"Will I now be host to botanical marvels?"
And recalled the hapless bush flamed
For Moses, the fig cursed by Jesus,
The thorn in Lourdes creaking into diffident

Bloom for Bernadette through mountain frost.
Was I in for armloads of lucious peaches
Or a pocket-display of selective blight,
The innocent switch smoked to jerky by sunset?
And how would I read either wondrous pole?
Would fruit mean *Praise. Continue as now?*
Would blight be the tangible verdict for *Turn*
Or *Wrong. Too late. Prepare to pay?*
How would I answer? Who would I tell?
A baffled week later I drove to the garden
Shop and chose the makings of a small
Commemoration—three dozen
Of the homeliest plants known to science,
All succulents: stonecrop, echeveria,
Aloes, sempervivums. The troll-woman
Ringing my purchases said "You're not
Expecting flowers from these?"

                                I said "Flowers
Never meant much to me."

                              "Me
Either," she whispered, "but that's a trade-
Secret."

                I promised silence and she warned me not
To eat them, "though they look good enough."
Home, I half-stripped; scooped
A bowl in the unnourished earth
By the peach, and set the green flesh
Of thirty-six low and blind-
Faced lives at the mercy of the site of his exit.

They've flourished, yes, but nothing prodigious—
Within two years under light care
From me, they'd filled their bed: huddled
And plump. Guests remark their oddness,
Their sturdy pluck in prospering on ground
Hospitable as sulfur. I offer no homily
On their local meaning, and no one's asked
For usable cuttings. The peachtree's holding
Its desperate own; I went once to move it

But stopped myself—if it means anything, it means
It *in place* (like ninety-eight percent of anything
Radiant). Since I live by a pond and its draining
Creek, I've met other snakes fairly often
In the time. Mostly harmless—red ratsnakes,
Kingsnakes, garters—they're asking only for sunning-
Space athwart my drive and the excess
Lesser reptilia to eat. Two weeks
Ago, I came on a large king
Resting at the chore of consuming a slightly
Thinner king—four inches of the vanquished
Neck were still free, apparently
Serene as a griddled saint—but the few
Black snakes are smaller than my visitant
And keep a skittish distance from the human
Zone. If his sons or avatars, they're plainly
Branded with the serpent curse, not spies
Or receptacles of my daily failure.
Me?—I poison my mice and harvest
Their frozen corpses from the crawl space before
They ripen. I work long days in near-
Solitude, am praised for my trick of making
The ecstasy of oneness look princely,
And sleep less each year—no dreams
I care to recall on rising.
                              I'm simply
The one happy man I know,
Assured of witness and judgment entirely
Beyond my power to guess or change—
Absent proprietor of gardens unthinkable
For beauty or pain.

WATCHMAN. TOWER. MIDNIGHT.

Twelve begins her frozen lucid chime
And in it each night's question—Do I to stay?
Am I required to man the striking time?

(Nineteen thousand shifts since thrust out free
From Mother's hot embalming rose blind dark,
Upright here alone and meant to see

The convex world pressed green beyond this glass,
The dazzling open faces bent my way
And balked by height, excluded, forced to pass

With only muffled calls, my signing hand
As earnest of a craving crater-stark:
A desert tower on the fruitful land.)

Silence. Midnight then. The instant gone.
Blood still floods these fingers, eyes still stare.
Agreed. And seated now, I hunt the dawn.

REYNOLDS PRICE

Born in Macon, North Carolina in 1933, Reynolds Price attended North Carolina schools and received his Bachelor of Arts degree from Duke University. As a Rhodes Scholar he studied for three years at Merton College, Oxford, receiving the Bachelor of Letters with a thesis on Milton. In 1958 he returned to Duke where he is now James B. Duke Professor of English. His first novel *A Long and Happy Life* appeared in 1962. A volume of stories *The Names and Faces of Heroes* appeared in 1963. In the years since, he has published *A Generous Man* (a novel), *Love and Work* (a novel), *Permanent Errors* (stories), *Things Themselves* (essays and scenes), *The Surface of Earth* (a novel), *Early Dark* (a play), *A Palpable God* (translations from the Bible with an essay on the origins and life of narrative), *The Source of Light* (a novel), *Vital Provisions* (poems), *Private Contentment* (a play), and *Kate Vaiden* (a novel). His first two novels and the story "A Chain of Love" are now collected in a single volume *Mustian*. His books have been translated into fourteen languages.